French for Little Boys

A beginning French workbook
for little boys

Written by: Yvonne Crawford
Illustrated by: Angelique Lackey

www.languageforlittlelearners.com

About this workbook

All people learn a foreign language best when they are properly motivated. This workbook is designed to target the obsessions of little boys: cars, trains, bugs, and more. You and your son will open the door to the French language while coloring trains, playing memory games with different types of bugs and racing his favorite toy car down an exciting race track full of obstacles.

This workbook is created especially for parents who do not have any prior knowledge of French. You and your son can embark on a journey of learning a foreign language together. Everything you need is inside this workbook, including a pronunciation guide, dictionary and teaching hints.

Every lesson will consist of a list of vocabulary words with pictures, three activities your son can do in the workbook with your guidance and two activities you can do together without the workbook for further practice. Each new word that is introduced will have its pronunciation next to it.

In the appendices there is a progress sheet for your child. When you and your child finish a lesson, turn to page 68 and have your child color a stepping stone. This will help your child to see, and take pride in his progress.

Do not put stress on your son to have perfect pronunciation or to remember every single word. If he forgets a word, simply repeat it and then use it in a sentence a few times; eventually he will catch on. It is important for him (and you) to have a positive first experience with learning a foreign language. It will encourage him to continue in the future with more language studies.

If your son is learning quickly, have him try the challenges that are placed throughout the workbook. They are designed for children who need and desire more language learning.

Table of Contents

Leçon 1
Hello Bugs!

Vocabulary:

l'abeille *lah-bay-ee*
bee

la cocinelle *lah-kok-see-nel*
ladybug

le papillon *luh-pa-pee-yoh*n
butterfly

la fourmi *lah-foor-mee*
ant

l'araignée *lah-ray-nyay*
spider

Fun Phrases:

bonjour	*bohn-zhuhr*	hello
au revoir	*oh-reh-vwahr*	good-bye
à bientôt	*a-byen-toh*	see you later

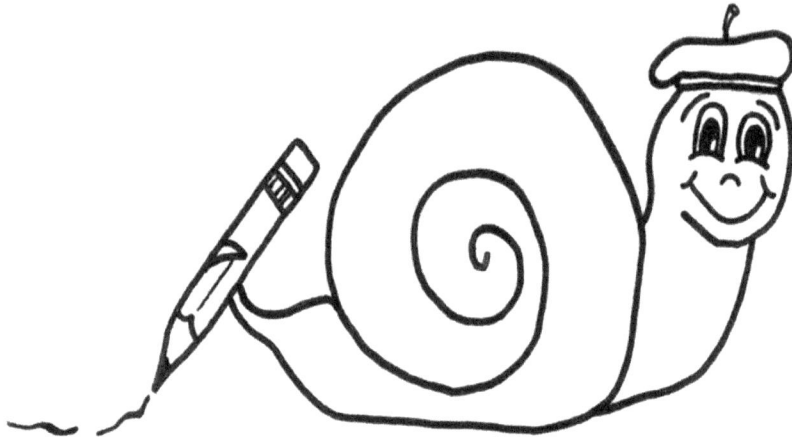

Teaching Tips:

- Throughout the day, point out the bugs that you see and ask your child what they are called in French. Before you know it your child will be making sentences like 'Look, there's a *papillon!*'

- There are many words in French in which you do not say the final letter or the last letter is barely heard. Refer to each word's pronuncation guide to see the proper pronunciation.

- If there is an *é* at the end of the word with an accent, you pronounce the 'e' as (*ay*) Otherwise, it is silent.

- Usually in French syllables are stressed the same.

Activité Une

Bonjour! My name is Pierre. I am an *escargot (ess-kahr-goh)* and I love to play games. Can you match the picture of each bug to its correct name?

le papillon

l'araignée

l'abeille

Activité Deux

Now you can greet each of my bug friends in French! For each picture above greet the bug, say 'Bonjour', then say the name of the bug.

Activité Trois

Can you help me match the baby bugs with their mothers? Every time you match two, make sure you say their names in French!

Activité Quatre

A Home for Bugs

What you will need:

a shoe box or jar
crayons
scissors
construction paper
tape or glue

What to do:

1. Take a shoe box or jar to create a bug house. Decorate your bug house with construction paper and crayons. You can even draw some bugs of your own on the outside, so the bugs will feel right at home. Make sure to cut some holes in the box, so the bugs can breathe.
2. With your parent, take your bug home to your backyard or to a park and find some bugs. Every time you find a bug, say its name in French.

Activité Cinq

Rock Bugs

What you will need:

a few flat rocks
paint
a paintbrush

What to do:

1. Paint each of the 5 bugs listed in this lesson on the rocks. As you paint them make sure you repeat their names in French.
2. After letting your rock bugs dry, ask a parent to hide them in your backyard, sand pit, or anywhere. Then, as you find each bug, tell your parent which bug you found in French.

Leçon 2
Polite Pets

Pierre's Pet Shop

le chien *luh-shee-uhn*
dog

le poisson *luh-pwah-sohn*
fish

le lapin *luh-lah-pahn*
rabbit

le chat *luh-shah*
cat

l'oiseau *lwah-zoh*
bird

Fun Phrases:

comment ça va?	koh-moh-sa-vah	how's it going?
ça va bien	sa-va-beeyen	It's going well
ça va mal	sa-va-mal	It's going poorly
comme-çi comme ça	kum-see-kum-sa	so-so
merci	mehr-see	thank you
de rien	duh-ree-yen	you're welcome
s'il vous plaît	seel-voo-play	please

Teaching Tips:

- Encourage your child to color all of the vocabulary page pictures. You can use this time to reinforce the new words. You and your child can repeat each word as he colors its corresponding picture.

- Remember to watch for signs that your child needs to take a break. You can always start where you left off tomorrow!

- Unlike in English, in French each sound is specifically spoken, so don't be afraid to really enunciate the sounds in French.

Activité Une

Come and meet my friends! Say *bonjour* to each animal. Next, draw a line from the animal to its favorite food. Your mom or dad can pretend to be the animal and say *merci* for thank you. You can reply *de rien* for "you're welcome" to each animal.

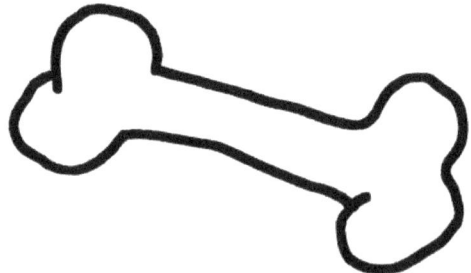

Activité Deux

Oh no, the pets in the pictures have no mouths! Will you draw mouths for each animal? Make two of the faces happy, one of the faces sad and one of the faces so-so. Then, when you are finished, ask the animal *Comment ça va?* and then pretend to be the animal and reply with ça *va bien*, ça *va mal* or *comme-çi comme-*ça. Use the following rabbits as an example.

Activité Trois

This is Pierre's favorite story about his visit to a pet store to pick out a pet. Your mom or dad can read the story to you, and whenever you see a picture in the story, say the word in French.

Pierre (l'escargot)	le chien	le lapin	le chat	le poisson	l'oiseau

Pierre's Trip to the Pet store

One day [snail] decided that he wanted a pet. He asked his mom if he could have one. She said, "Okay [snail], you may have one. Let's go to the pet store and pick one out." They went to the pet store and the first animal they saw was a big [dog]. [snail] jumped up and down and said "I want a [dog]". His mom replied "I'm sorry [snail], [dog] is too big for our house, you need something smaller." He immediately found another pet that he liked. "Mom I would like this [bird], s'il vous plaît." His mom looked at the [bird] and imagined it tweeting all night. "I'm sorry, that [bird] is too loud, find a pet that is quieter." [snail] looked and looked, then he saw a [rabbit].
"I want this [rabbit]. He's so quiet," [snail] said.

16

Mom looked at the mess that the 🐰 had made in his cage and she said "I'm sorry dear, he is too messy. You need to find a pet that is cleaner." 🐌 saw a 🐱 licking himself and he said, "A Mom? I think they are very clean." "Oh 🐌 ", Mom said sadly, "I love cats, but the fur makes me sneeze, ah ah ah chooo!" 🐌 was about to give up when he saw a 🐟 swimming around in a bowl. He thought to himself, before he told his mom, The 🐟 is not too big like a 🐕 . It does not make too much noise, like a 🐤 . It is not too messy, like a 🐰 . It does not have fur that makes mom sneeze, like a 🐱 . Maybe this pet might work. "Mom," 🐌 asked tentatively, "Can I have a 🐟 ?" "Of course", mom replied. Pierre and his mom went home with his new pet 🐟 .

Fin - The End

Teaching Tips:

- You can repeat this story several times over the course of this book to reinforce the names of animals in French.

Activité Quatre

Be Polite

Throughout the day, use your French! When you would like something from your mom or dad, say *s'il vous plaît.* The most important word is *merci* for thank you. Also, there is *de rien* for you're welcome. Every time you say one of these polite expressions today, you can come back to this workbook and record it on this page. Color a star for each time you use one of your new French phrases.

s'il vous plaît   **merci**   **de rien**

☆ ☆ ☆ ☆ ☆ ☆ ☆ ☆ ☆

Activité Cinq

Faces

What you will need:
construction paper
markers/crayons
scissors

What to do:
1. With your mom's or dad's help, cut out three big circles.
2. Draw a face in each circle. Make sure to include eyes, a nose, ears, and hair on each of the three circles.
3. Now, draw a smiley mouth on one circle, a frown on one circle and a so-so face on the last circle. As you are drawing the mouths, repeat the phrases in French ç*a va mal*, ç*a va bien* and *comme-çi comme-ça*.
4. Take a large piece of construction paper, tape all of the faces onto it, and hang it on the fridge.
5. Throughout the day, go to the faces and practice saying "How are you?" in French by saying *Comment* ç*a va?,* then you can point to the face that shows how you feel, and say the phrase in French.

Leçon 3

Truckin' through Numbers

Vocabulary:

la voiture *lah-vwa-tur*
car

le camion *luh-ka-mee-on*
truck

la moto *lah-moh-toh*
motorcycle

la bicyclette *lah-bee-see-klet*
bicycle

1 **un** *uhn*
one

2 **deux** *deuh*
two

3 **trois** *trwah*
three

4 **quatre** *katr*
four

5 **cinq** *sank*
five

Teaching Tips:

- In order to reinforce learning the numbers, use the French numbers throughout the day. Whenever your child says a number in English, ask them to say it in French as well.

- Add an 's' to the end of a noun to make it plural, which is silent.
  une moto - one motorcycle
  deux motos - two motorcycles

Activité Une

Count the different vehicles in French, then write the number in the box.

Activité Deux

This old *camion* needs some new tires. Circle the stack with *quatre* tires.

Challenge:

Take a few toasted oat cereal rings and stack the "tires" in amounts ranging from one to five. Count the number of tires in each stack in French.

Activité Trois

Follow the path of each vehicle and find out which one leads to me!

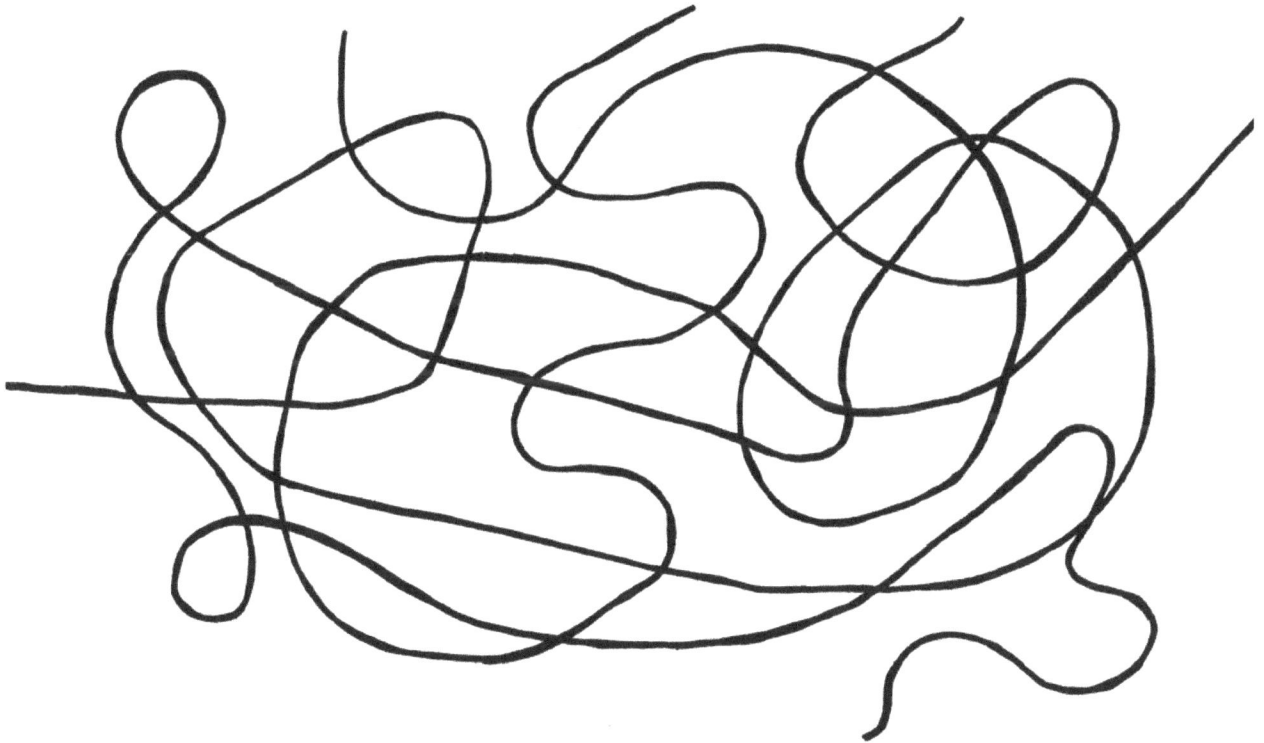

Activité Quatre

Counting Cars

Gather five of your toy *voitures* and *camions*, then count them. Say phrases like: *cinq voitures* and *deux camions* as you play with them. You can also practice being polite by sharing your cars with your parents. When you give them a car, they can say *merci* and you can reply *de rien*.

Activité Cinq

Car Scrapbook

What you will need:

old magazines or old car brochures
newspaper advertisements
construction paper
glue
scissors
a hole punch
yarn
crayons

What to do:

1. Look through the magazines and brochures. Find pictures of cars and trucks that you like.
2. Repeat their names in French as you cut them out.
3. Fold a piece of construction paper in half and glue your pictures on all parts of the paper.
4. After you finish finding cars and trucks for your scrapbook, have your parents help you punch holes in it on one side, thread a piece of yarn through the holes, and then tie the yarn in order to bind your book.
5. Finally, decorate your book by coloring it.

Leçon 4
Colors

Vocabulary:

vert *vehr*
green

bleu *bluh*
blue

rouge *roozh*
red

jaune *zhohn*
yellow

noir *nuahr*
black

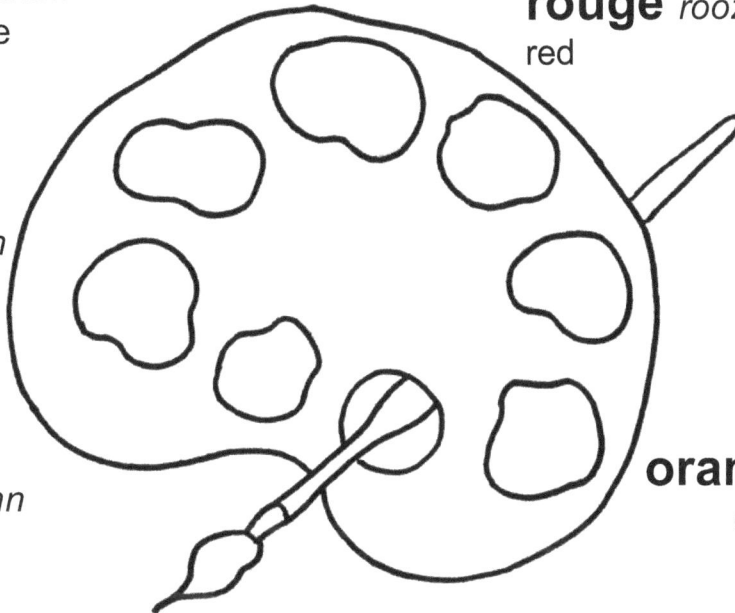

blanc *blahn*
white

orange *or-ahnj*
orange

Fun Phrases:

je m'appelle	zhu-mah-pehl	my name is
comment t'appelles-tu?	koh-moh-tah-pehl-too	what is your name?
et	ay	and

Teaching tips:
- Most adjectives in French follow the noun, for example:
    la voiture bleue - the blue car
    le camion vert - the green truck

Challenge:
- You can also ask this question to your child to reinforce colors.
    Quelle couleur? *kehl-koo-lehr* - which color?

Activité Une

Let's color my animal friends. Use the key to color the different animals.

l'oiseau	vert
le chien	bleu
le chat	orange
le poisson	noir et vert
le lapin	jaune

Activité Deux

Color the vehicles below different colors and say their names in French.

Challenge:

Use *Il y a* (eel ee ah) which means "there is/there are" to explain to your parents what is happening in this picture.

> *Il y a une voiture rouge.* - There is a red car.
> *Il y a un camion bleu.* - There is a blue truck.

Activité Trois

Use the frame below and draw a picture of yourself. Write your name at the bottom after *Je m'appelle* and show your mom and dad that you can say "My name is…" in French.

Je m'appelle _____.

Activité Quatre

Rainbow Rice

What you will need:

rice
food coloring
a plastic container with a lid

What to do:

1. Take the bag of rice and pour it into the plastic container
2. Spread the rice evenly in the container.
3. Pick up each bottle of food coloring, and practice saying the names of the colors in French.
4. With your mom or dad's help, pour the different colors of food coloring into separate sections of the rice. Try not to mix them up so that you will have nice vibrant colors.
5. Allow the rice to dry for at least 1 hour.
6. Now, you can play with your special new colored rice. As you play you can talk about the different colors. You can also drive your toy cars through it and make mountains of colored rice for them to climb over. Have fun with it!

Activité Cinq

Hello Friends

What you will need:

Your favorite toys with names (if they don't have names, now may be the time to name them) - trains, stuffed animals, anything…

What to do:

1. Line up all of your toys and ask the first toy "Comment t'appelles-tu?" which means "What is your name?"
2. Then, reply for your toy (in a different voice) "Je m'appelle…"
3. Continue with the rest of your toys doing the same thing.

Leçon 5
Flying with More Numbers

Vocabulary:

le cerf-volant
luh-ser-voh-lahn
kite

la montgolfière
lah-mohn-gohl-fee-ehr
hot air balloon

la fusée
lah-foo-zay
rocket

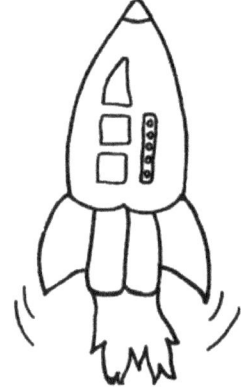

l'hélicoptère
lay-lee-kop-tehr
helicopter

l'avion
lah-vee-yohn
airplane

six *sees*
six
6

sept *seht*
seven
7

huit *weet*
eight
8

neuf *neuhf*
nine
9

dix *dees*
ten
10

Activité Une

Bonjour! Look at the picture below. Can you help me find all of the avions, cerf-volants, montgolfières, fusées, and hélicoptères? Each time you find one, use your French. Say 'I see a ...' or 'Je vois un...' When you find one, color it! And at the end you can count all of the high flyers that you have colored!

Activité Deux

Pierre has drawn a picture for you, but he has forgotten to connect some of the dots. Use your crayon and connect all of the dots to finish his picture. As you connect the dots say each number in French!

1

10

3

2

4

5

8

7

6

9

Activité Trois

Count the pictures below in French, and then circle the correct number.

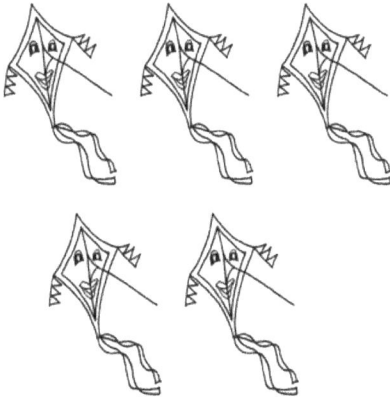

| 5 | 6 | 7 |

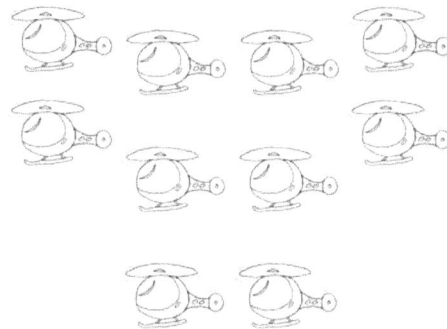

| 8 | 10 | 9 |

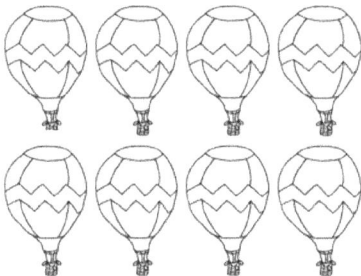

| 7 | 9 | 8 |

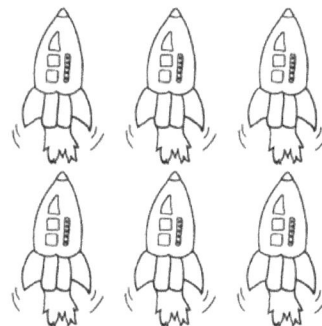

| 7 | 6 | 5 |

Challenge:

Start a collection of objects! Brainstorm with your parent about different things that could be in your collection (toy cars, rocks, sea shells, pencils, stamps, postcards). After gathering the objects for your collection, count the number of items in your collection in French.

Activité Quatre

To the Moon...

What you will need:

constuction paper
empty toilet paper rolls
crayons or markers
tape or glue
scissors

What to do:

1. Imagine you are going to the moon. What kind of spaceship would you like to take you there?
2. Using all of the supplies, create a rocket ship from your imagination.
3. After you have completed your space ship, now you can launch it. Say your count down in French 5-4-3-2-1... *Bon voyage!* Have a good trip!

Activité Cinq

Kites!

What you will need:

construction paper
crayons
yarn
scissors
glue

What to do:

1. Using one piece of construction paper, cut out a diamond shape to make your kite.
2. Decorate your kite by coloring different shapes and designs.
3. Cut a piece of yarn for the tail of your kite.
4. Cut small pieces of construction paper to be the ribbons on the tail of your kite. Then, attach the tail to the kite with glue.
5. After waiting for your kite to dry, hang your kite from the ceiling or high on the wall. When you see it, say *"le cerf-volant!"*

Leçon 6

Robots

Vocabulary:

le robot *luh-roh-boh*
robot

la tête *lah-teht*
head

la main *lah-meh$_n$*
hand

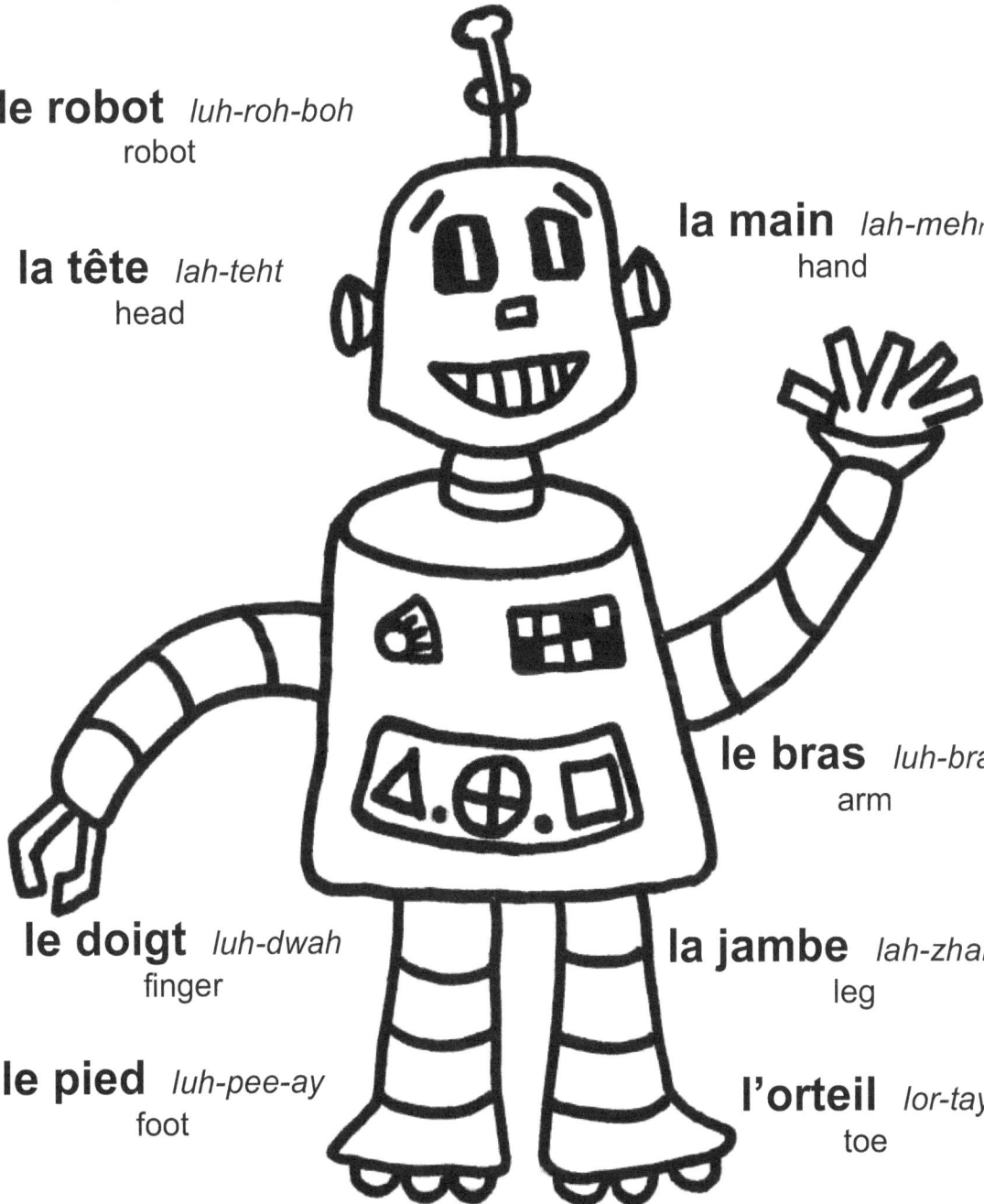

le bras *luh-brah*
arm

le doigt *luh-dwah*
finger

la jambe *lah-zhahmb*
leg

le pied *luh-pee-ay*
foot

l'orteil *lor-tay*
toe

Fun Phrases:

j'ai	zhay	I have
tu as	too-ah	you have

Teaching Tips:

- It's important to review previous lessons to make sure your child remembers other words he has learned.

Challenge:

- Use this question word to help your child practice numbers in French:

combien	kom-beeyen	how much / how many

Activité Une

Let's build a robot! Below are the bodies and heads of two robots, use your crayons to draw *jambes, mains, doigts,* and all other parts of the robot. As you draw each body part, say the word in French.

Activité Deux

Look at the different pictures of robots. In each row find the one robot that is different from the other two and tell your parent which body part is different, in French.

Activité Trois

Say these words in French and then draw a line from each word to its matching picture.

la jambe   le bras   le doigt   la tête

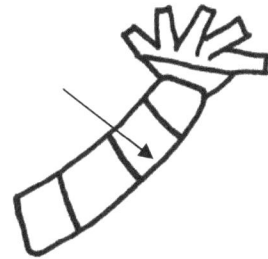
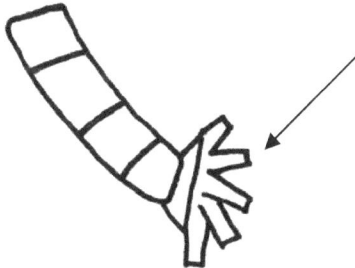
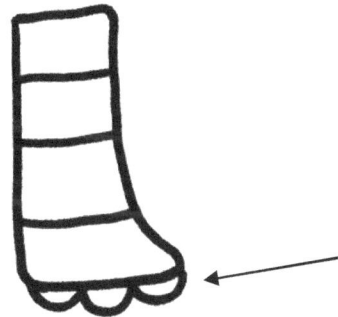

Challenge:

Sing and act out the "Hokey Pokey" song with your child using the French term for each body part focus on in this lesson. You can sing the song in English and say the body parts in French. For example: "You put your right *jambe* in. You put your right *jambe* out. You put your right *jambe* in and you shake it all about. You do the hokey pokey and you turn yourself around. That's what it's all about!"

Activité Quatre
Making Robots

What you will need:

Modeling clay

What to do:

1. Make robot body parts together with your mom or dad. As you finish making each body part say the name and color of it in French. For example: *la tête rouge*
2. Build some robots. After you have built a few robots, you can pretend to be a robot and speak to your mom or dad. You can say things like *Bonjour* and *Comment ça va?*

Challenge:

You can also describe what you see:

je vois	zhe-vwah	I see

Je vois une jambe rouge. I see a red leg.

Activité Cinq
A Paper Me

What you will need:

freezer paper
crayons
scissors

What to do:

1. Roll out a big sheet of freezer paper on the floor - about the size of yourself.
2. Have your mom or dad trace your body onto the paper.
3. Draw and color your hair, face and clothes.
4. Ask your mom or dad to help cut out your picture of yourself and then hang it on a wall or door.
5. Point to all of your body parts on the picture and say their names in French.

Leçon 7

All Aboard!

Vocabulary:

la locomotive *lah-loh-koh-moh-teev*
engine

le train *luh-treh*
the train

le tender *luh-tehn-duhr*
tender

la voiture *lah-vwa-tur*
passenger car

les rails du train
*lay-rayls-doo-treh*n
train tracks

le wagon de queue
luh-vah-gon-du-koo
caboose

le wagon *luh-vah-gon*
boxcar

41

Fun Phrases:

ici	ee-see	here
là	lah	there
je vois	zhu-vwah	I see
tu vois	too-vwah	you see

Challenge:

- If your child is ready, you can teach him how to form a question in French. Simply add *Est-ce que* to the beginning of any sentence. Below are some examples:

  ***Tu vois une locomotive.* You see an engine.**

  ***Est-ce que tu vois une locomotive?* Do you see an engine?**

  Il y a deux wagon de queues. There are 2 cabooses.

  Est-ce qu'il y a deux wagon de queues? Are there 2 cabooses?

- Remember to teach these lessons as slowly or as quickly as your child needs. If your child is not ready for this challenge, you can always come back to it at a later time.

Activité Une

Uh oh, this train is uncoupled! Can you number the pieces of the train to show which order they should be in? When you number a piece, make sure you say the number in French and the name of the train car or engine in French!

Activité Deux

This little steam engine has lost his whistle. Read this story with your parent's help to see what happens. If he says a word in French, point to it in the picture on the next page.

Once upon a time there was a little steam *locomotive,* who was very sad because he couldn't find his whistle. He traveled along the tracks searching for it. The first thing he saw was a *chien.* He wished he could toot his whistle and say *bonjour,* but he remembered he had lost his whistle. So, the little steam *locomotive* traveled onward.

Next, the little steam *locomotive* saw something shiny and thought it was his whistle, but it was not. It was his friend the *robot.* He wanted to toot his whistle and say *bonjour,* but he couldn't, so he continued down the tracks looking for his whistle.

The little steam *locomotive* continued and heard a sound, but it wasn't the right sound. Again, he wanted to toot his whistle to say *bonjour,* but he couldn't. It was his friend Pierre honking the horn in his *voiture.* The little *locomotive* continued on his search for his whistle.

Finally, after searching and searching, the little steam *locomotive* found his whistle. The conductor attached it to the *locomotive* and they went back the way they came from. The steam *locomotive* passed Pierre in his *voiture* and he tooted his horn *un* time. Then, he passed his friend the *robot* and tooted his horn *deux* times. Lastly, he passed a *chien* and tooted his horn *trois* times and before heading back to the engine shed for a rest.

Now try to tell the story yourself or make up your own story. Start at the train and follow along the tracks. As you pass each picture, make sure you say their name in French!

Activité Trois

Hmmmm...a few things are just a bit different, but what? Find the nine differences between the two pictures below. Count the differences in French.

Activité Quatre

Make Your Own Cargo Train

What you will need:

shoe box
construction paper
crayons or markers
glue or tape
scissors
string/yarn

What to do:

1. Take the lid off of the shoe box, or cut the top off.
2. Use your imagination and decorate the shoe box to make it look like a train. Attach a string to the end of the train, so you can pull it.
3. Now, you need to take your new train on a delivery trip. Find things you have that you can deliver to your mom or dad. You can tell them what the colors of the items are in French, when you deliver them.

Activité Cinq

Toys

What you will need:

Some of your toy trains, cars, planes, animals, etc. (Use can use anything that we have learned the name of in a previous lesson.)

What to do:

1. Sit down with your mom and dad to play this game.
2. She will say in *J'ai*....and then select 1 toy. Then you say *Tu as...* and then the name of the toy.
3. Continue until you both have named all of your toys.

For example:
Your mom might say: *J'ai une voiture.*
You would reply: *Tu as une voiture.*

Leçon 8
At the Zoo

Vocabulary:

le lion *luh-lee-oh*
lion

l'éléphant
lay-lay-fan
elephant

l'ours *loors*
bear

la girafe *lah-gee-rahf*
giraffe

le zèbre *luh-zeh-br*
zebra

le tigre *luh-tee-gr*
tiger

le zoo luh-zoh
zoo

Fun Phrases:

petit(e)	peh-tee (peh-teet)	small
grand(e)	grahn_d (grahnd)	big
lent(e)	lehn (lehnt)	slow
rapide	rah-peed	fast
je suis	zhuh-swee	I am
tu es	too-eh	you are

Teaching Tips:
- As you have learned, most adjectives in French go after the noun; however, some adjectives in French go before the noun, such as *petit* and *grand*.

    le petit chat - the little cat

Activité Une

Ooh la la! The animals have escaped from their pens! Can you draw a line between the animals and their correct pens? Remember to say the animal's name in French as you draw the line.

le zèbre

l'ours

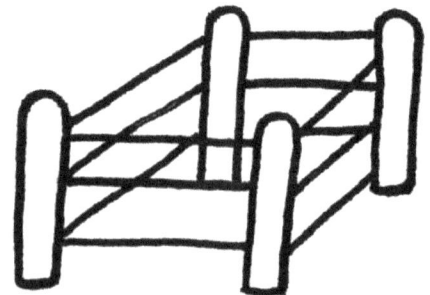

l'éléphant

Activité Deux

Look at all of the different animals on this page. Some are *grand* and some are very *petit*. Using your crayons or markers, draw a *rouge* circle around all of the *grand* animals. Draw a *vert* circle around all of the *petit* animals.

Activité Trois

Uh oh...the animals are all mixed up! Look at each picture and say which parts of each animal make up this new animal. In the empty box, create your own mixed up animal. Then, describe all of the mixed up animals to your parents in French. Remember to use the names of the body parts you have learned!

Activité Quatre
Animal Parade

What you will need:
paper plates
crayons
scissors
construction paper
glue

What to do:
1. Create your own animal mask by using the materials listed. You can also make a tail for yourself.
2. Have an animal parade around your house. Make sure you say *Je suis... (I am)* to let everyone know which animal you are. For example: *Je suis un tigre.* (I am a tiger.)

Activité Cinq
Animal Charades

What you will need:
strips of paper
a cup
a pencil

What to do:
1. Ask your mom or dad to write the names or draw pictures of the animals from this chapter on strips of paper.
2. Fold up the strips of paper and put them in the cup.
3. Take turns with your mom or dad taking a piece of paper from the cup and pretending to be that animal. Try not to make sounds or use words when acting out your animal. Make sure to guess the animal name in French.

Leçon 9
Slimy Friends

Vocabulary:

la limace *lah-lee-mahs*
slug

le serpent *luh-sehr-pehn*
snake

l'escargot *lehs-cahr-go*
snail

la grenouille
lah-greh-noo-ee
frog

la chenille *lah-chehn-ee*
caterpillar

Fun Phrases:

j'aime	zhaym	I like
tu aimes	too-aym	you like

Teaching Tips:

When a word that ends with a vowel is followed by a word that begins with a vowel, the first vowel is dropped and an apostrophe is added. For example:

je + aime = j'aime
le + escargot = l'escargot

Challenge:

You can have your son practice saying things he likes with plural nouns. If a noun is either feminine or masculine the plural for "the" is *les*. He can practice phrases like:

J'aime les serpents.
J'aime les lions.

Activité Une

Snakes and Ladders

What you will need:

a die

a counter for each player, for example a small plastic animal or toy car

Vocabulary:

commence	koh-mahns	start
fin	feh	end

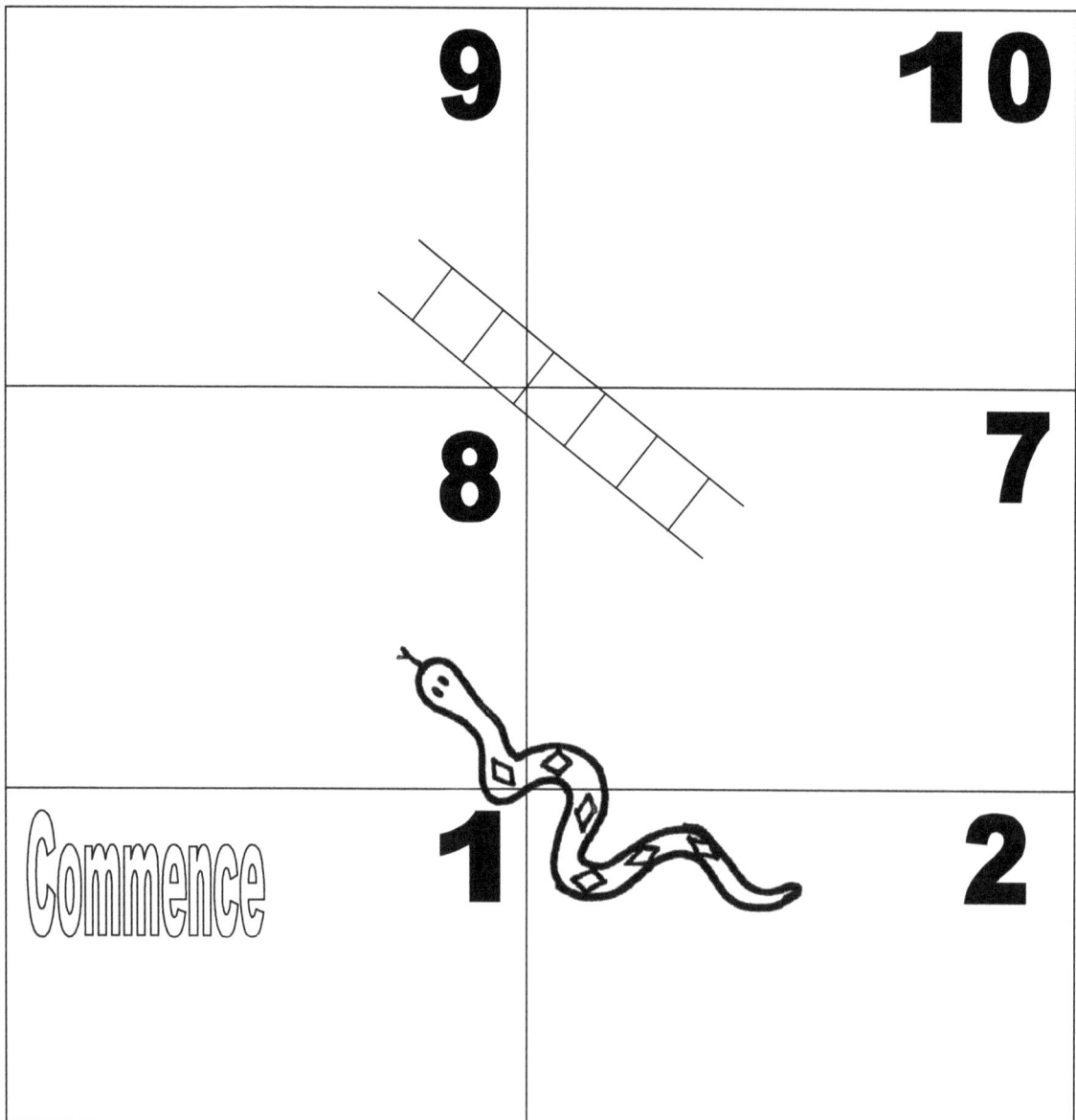

How to Play:

1. The youngest person goes first. Roll the die and then move that many spaces. Count in French as you move your counter.
2. If you land on a *serpent*, you have to slide down it and land on the square at the end of its body.
3. If you land on a ladder, you can climb up to the square it ends on.
4. The first person to reach the finish (*fin*) is the winner!

Bonne chance! Good luck!

11	**12** Fin
6	**5**
3	**4**

Activité Deux

These animals have lost their friends; match each pair of animals and then say their names in French.

Activité Trois

L'escargot, Pierre, wants to go home. As he passes friends on the road, say in French each animal's name and the other things he sees. Say *il voit*…Then, color the picture using the color key below.

color key	
l'avion	noir
le tigre	orange
le chien	rouge
le zébre	vert

Activité Quatre

Caterpillar Friends

What you will need:

cotton balls
acrylic paint
scissors
paper
glue

What to do:

1. Have your mom or dad help you draw and cut the shape of a caterpillar out of paper.
2. Dip your cotton balls into different colors of paint and let them dry.
3. Glue your cotton balls onto the paper and create a very colorful caterpillar. After you let it dry you can hang it on your fridge. Every time you go to the fridge, point to the different colors and say their names in French.

Activité Cinq

I Like...

What you will need:

construction paper
crayons

What to do:

1. Take a piece of construction paper and at the top write *j'aime* on it. You can ask your mom or dad to help you.
2. Draw all of the things that *tu aimes*. They could be people, toys, places; anything that *tu aimes*.
3. Show your mom and dad your artwork and tell them all of the things that *tu aimes*.

Leçon 10

Rescue Vehicles

Vocabulary:

la depanneuse
lah-deh-pahn-nuhz
tow truck

l'ambulance
lahm-boo-lahns
ambulance

la voiture de police
lah-vwah-tur-duh-poh-lees
police car

le camion de pompier
luh-ka-mee-on-duh-pohm-pee-eh
fire truck

Challenge:
- To create a negative sentence in French, put 'ne' before the verb and 'pas' after the verb. For example:
  Je ne vois pas la voiture de police.
  I don't see the police car.

Activité Une

My favorite rescue vehicle is *le camion de pompier*. Which of these rescue vehicles is your favorite? Draw a circle around all of the rescue vehicles you like. As you draw the circle say: '*J'aime* _____'.

Activité Deux

Pierre is late for his job at the quarry. Help him follow the path so he can get there as soon as possible. As you pass the different types of vehicles make sure you say their names in French. Also, you can draw your own rescue vehicles on the picture!

Activité Trois

Pierre needs your help to put out all of the little fires. Color all of the fires *orange* or *rouge* and as you color them count how many fires there are in French. Afterwards put out the fires by coloring the water *bleu* from the hose.

Activité Quatre

Memory

You will need:
the memory cards found in the appendix of this book.

What to do:
1. Shuffle the cards.
2. Turn all of the cards upside down in rows in front of you on a table or on the floor.
3. Pick up 2 and see if they match. As you pick up each card, remember to say each picture's name in French. If they match, you can keep those cards and continue with your turn. If they do not match, put them back upside-down and then it will be the next player's turn.
4. The player with the most pairs of matched cards wins.

Challenge: You can vary the level of difficulty of this game by using some or all of the pairs of cards.

Activité Cinq

My Favorite Rescue Vehicle

You will need:
a medium sized box (an old diaper box would work perfectly)
crayons
construction paper
scissors
glue

What to do:
1. Have your mom or dad cut out the bottom and top of the box.
2. Decorate the box as your favorite rescue vehicle.
3. Step inside your rescue vehicle—hold onto the side and off you go! Remember to say what vehicle you are driving in French as you play in your rescue vehicle. For example: *Je suis une voiture de police.*

Appendices

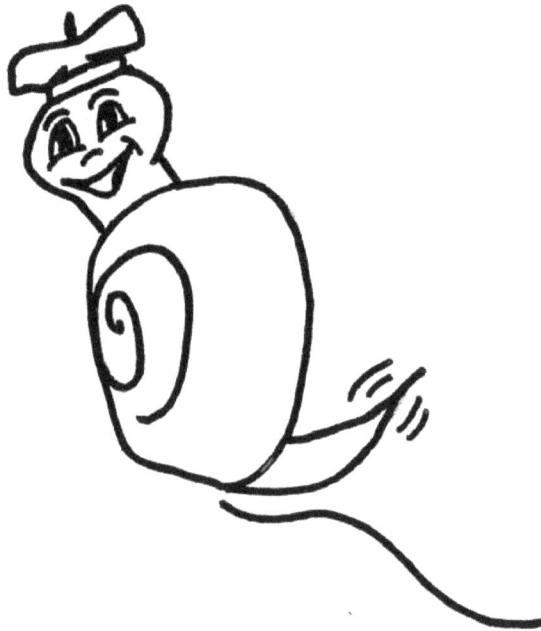

My French Path

Every time you finish a leçon in the book,
color a stone until you reach Pierre.

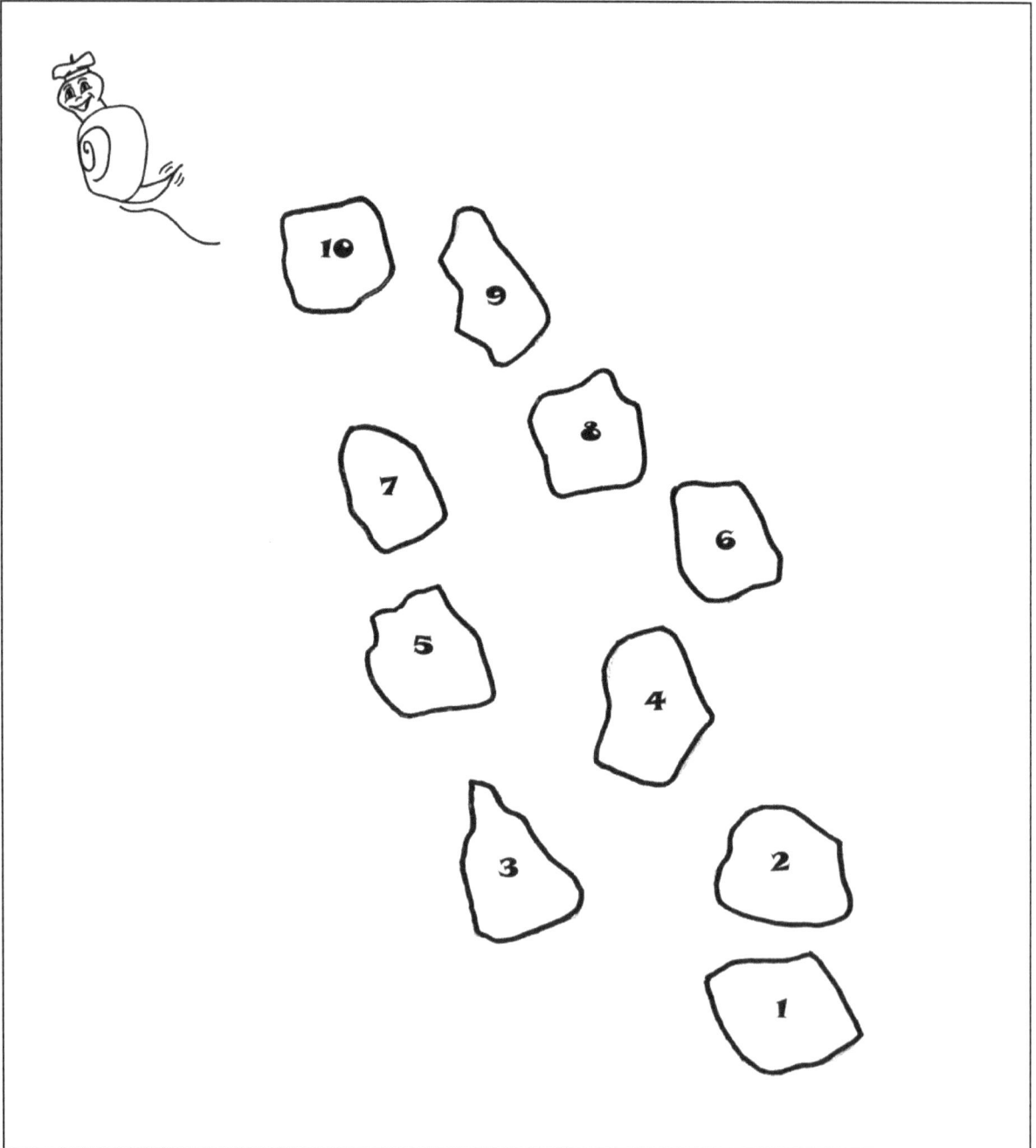

10
9
8
7
6
5
4
3
2
1

Three cheers for

_____

Félicitations!
Congratulations!
You have successfully finished
French for Little Boys.
You did a wonderful job!

English to French Dictionary

a(n)	un(e)	*uhn (oon)*
airplane	l'avion (m)	*lah-vee-yohn*
ambulance	l'ambulance (f)	*lahm-boo-lahns*
and	et	*ay*
ant	la fourmi	*lah-foor-mee*
arm	le bras	*luh-brah*
bear	l'ours (m)	*loors*
bee	l'abeille (f)	*lah-bay-ee*
bicycle	la bicyclette	*lah-bee-see-klet*
big	grand(e)	*grahnd (grahnd)*
bird	l'oiseau (m)	*lwah-zoh*
black	noir	*nuahr*
blue	bleu	*bluh*

box car	le wagon	*luh-vah-gon*
butterfly	le papillon	*luh-pa-pee-yohn*
caboose	le wagon de queue	*luh-vah-gon-du-koo*
car	la voiture	*lah-vwa-tur*
cat	le chat	*luh-shah*
caterpillar	la chenille	*lah-chehn-ee*
color	la couleur	*lah-koo-lehr*
congratulations	félicitations	*feh-li-si-tay-shohn*
dog	le chien	*luh-shee-uhn*
eight	huit	*weet*
elephant	l'éléphant (m)	*lay-lay-fan*
end	fin	*feh*
engine	la locomotive	*lah-loh-koh-moh-teev*
fast	rapide	*rah-peed*

finger	le doigt	*luh-dwah*
fire truck	la camion de pompiers	*luh-ka-mee-on-duh-pohm-pee-eh*
fish	le poisson	*luh-pwah-sohn*
five	cinq	*sank*
foot	le pied	*luh-pee-ay*
four	quatre	*katr*
frog	la grenouille	*lah-greh-noo-ee*
giraffe	la girafe	*lah-gee-rahf*
good-bye	au revoir	*oh-reh-vwahr*
good luck	bonne chance	*bohn-chahns*
green	vert	*vehr*
hand	la main	*lah-mehn*
have a good trip	bon voyage	*boh-voy-azj*
head	la tête	*lah-teht*

helicopter	l'hélicoptère (m)	lay-lee-kop-tehr
hello	bonjour	bohn-zhuhr
here	ici	ee-see
hot air balloon	la montgolfière	lah-mohn-gohl-fee-ehr
how is it going?	comment ça va?	koh-moh-sa-vah
how many? / how much?	combien?	kom-beeyen
I am	je suis	zhuh-swee
I have	j'ai	zhay
I like	j'aime	zhaym
I see	je vois	zhe-vwah
it's going poorly	ça va mal	sa-va-mal
it's going well	ça va bien	sa-va-beeyen
kite	le cerf-volant	luh-ser-voh-lahn

lady bug	la cocinelle	*lah-kok-see-nel*
leg	la jambe	*lah-zhahmb*
lesson	la leçon	*lah-les-sohn*
lion	le lion	*luh-lee-oh*
motorcycle	la moto	*lah-moh-toh*
my name is	je m'appelle...	*zhu-mah-pehl*
not (negative)	ne...pas	*nuh...pah*
nine	neuf	*n*euhf
one	un(e)	*uh*n *( )*
orange	orange	*or-ahnj*
passenger car	voiture	*lah-vwa-tur*
please	s'il vous plaît	*seel-voo-play*
police car	la voiture de po-lice	*lah-vwah-tur-duh-poh-lees*
rabbit	le lapin	*luh-lah-pah*n

red	rouge	*roozh*
robot	le robot	*luh-roh-boh*
rocket	la fusée	*lah-foo-zay*
see you later	à bientôt	*a-byen-toh*
seven	sept	*seht*
six	six	*sees*
slow	lent(e)	*lehn (lehnt)*
slug	la limace	*lah-lee-mahs*
small	petit(e)	*peh-tee (peh-teet)*
snail	l'escargot (m)	*lehs-cahr-go*
snake	le serpent	*luh-sehr-pehn*
so-so	comme-çi comme-ça	*kum-see-kum-sa*
spider	l'araignée (f)	*lah-ray-nyay*
start	commence	*koh-mahns*

ten	dix	*dees*
tender	le tender	*luh-tehn-duhr*
thank you	merci	mehr-see
there	là	*lah*
there is/there are	Il y a	*eel-ee-ah*
three	trois	*trwah*
tiger	le tigre	*luh-tee-gr*
toe	l'orteil (m)	*lor-tay*
tow truck	la depanneuse	*lah-deh-pahn-nuhz*
train	le train	*luh-treh*
train track	les rails du train	*lay-rayls-doo-trehn*
truck	le camion	*luh-ka-mee-on*
two	deux	*deuh*
what is you name?	comment t'ap-pelles-tu?	*koh-moh-tah-pehl-too*

which	quel(le)	*kehl*
white	blanc	*blahn*
yellow	jaune	*zhohn*
you are	tu es	*too-eh*
you're welcome	de rien	*duh-ree-yen*
you have	tu as	*too-ah*
you like	tu aimes	*too-aym*
you see	tu vois	*too-vwah*
zebra	le zèbre	*luh-zeh-br*
zoo	le zoo	*luh-zoh*

French to English Dictionary

à bientôt	*a-byen-toh*	see you later
l'abeille (f)	*lah-bay-ee*	bee
l'ambulance (f)	*lahm-boo-lahns*	ambulance
l'araignée (f)	*lah-ray-nyay*	spider
au revoir	*oh-reh-vwahr*	good-bye
l'avion (m)	*lah-vee-yohn*	airplane
la bicyclette	*lah-bee-see-klet*	bicycle
blanc	*blahn*	white
bleu	*bluh*	blue
bon voyage	*boh-voy-azj*	have a good trip
bonne chance	*bohn-chahns*	good luck
bonjour	*bohn-zhuhr*	hello
le bras	*luh-brah*	arm

le camion	*luh-ka-mee-on*	truck
la camion de pompiers	*luh-ka-mee-on-duh-pohm-pee-eh*	fire truck
le cerf-volant	*luh-ser-voh-lahn*	kite
le chat	*luh-shah*	cat
la chenille	*lah-chehn-ee*	caterpillar
le chien	*luh-shee-uhn*	dog
cinq	*sank*	five
la cocinelle	*lah-kok-see-nel*	lady bug
combien?	*kom-beeyen*	how many? / how much?
comment ça va?	*koh-moh-sa-vah*	how is it going?
comme-çi comme-ça	*kum-see-kum-sa*	so-so
commence	*koh-mahns*	start
comment t'ap-pelles-tu?	*koh-moh-tah-pehl-too*	what is your name?
la couleur	*lah-koo-lehr*	color

ça va bien	*sa-va-beeyen*	it's going well
ça va mal	*sa-va-mal*	it's going poorly
de rien	*duh-ree-yen*	you're welcome
la depanneuse	*lah-deh-pahn-nuhz*	tow truck
deux	*deuh*	two
dix	*dees*	ten
le doigt	*luh-dwah*	finger
l'éléphant (m)	*lay-lay-fan*	elephant
l'escargot (m)	*lehs-cahr-go*	snail
et	*ay*	and
félicitations	*feh-li-si-tay-shohn*	congratulations
fin	*feh*	*end*
la fourmi	*lah-foor-mee*	ant

la fusée	*lah-foo-zay*	rocket
la girafe	*lah-gee-rahf*	giraffe
grand(e)	*grahnd (grahnd)*	big
la grenouille	*lah-greh-noo-ee*	frog
l'hélicoptère (m)	*lay-lee-kop-tehr*	helicopter
huit	*weet*	eight
ici	*ee-see*	here
il y a	*eel-ee-ah*	there is/there are
j'ai	*zhay*	I have
j'aime	*zhaym*	I like
la jambe	*lah-zhahmb*	leg
jaune	*zhohn*	yellow
je m'appelle	*zhu-mah-pehl*	my name is
je suis	*zhuh-swee*	I am

je vois	zhe-vwah	I see
là	lah	there
le lapin	luh-lah-pahn	rabbit
leçon	lah-les-sohn	lesson
lent(e)	lehn (lehnt)	slow
la limace	lah-lee-mahs	slug
le lion	luh-lee-oh	lion
la locomotive	lah-loh-koh-moh-teev	engine
la main	lah-teht	hand
merci	mehr-see	thank you
la montgolfière	lah-mohn-gohl-fee-ehr	hot-air balloon
la moto	lah-moh-toh	motocycle
ne...pas	nuh...pah	not (negative)
neuf	neuhf	nine

noir	*nuahr*	black
l'oiseau (m)	*lwah-zoh*	bird
orange	*or-ahnj*	orange
l'orteil (m)	*lor-tay*	toe
l'ours (m)	*loors*	bear
le papillon	*luh-pa-pee-yohn*	butterfly
petit(e)	*peh-tee (pehteet)*	small
le pied	*luh-pee-ay*	foot
le poisson	*luh-pwah-sohn*	fish
quatre	*katr*	four
quel(le)	*kehl*	which
rapide	*rah-peed*	fast
les rails du train	*lay-rayls-doo-trehn*	train track
le robot	*luh-roh-boh*	robot

rouge	*roozh*	red
sept	*seht*	seven
le serpent	*luh-sehr-pehn*	snake
s'il vous plaît	*seel-voo-play*	please
six	*sees*	six
le tender	*luh-tehn-duhr*	tender
la tête	*lah-teht*	head
le tigre	*luh-tee-gr*	tiger
le train	*luh-treh*	train
trois	*trwah*	three
tu aimes	*too-aym*	you like
tu as	*too-ah*	you have
tu es	*too-eh*	you are
tu vois	*too-vwah*	you see

un(e)	*uhn (oon)*	one / a(n)
vert	*vehr*	green
la voiture	*lah-vwa-tur*	car / passenger car
la voiture de police	*lah-vwah-tur-duh-pol-lees*	police car
le wagon	*luh-vah-gon*	box car
le wagon de queue	*luh-vah-gon-du-koo*	caboose
le zèbre	*luh-zeh-br*	zebra
le zoo	*luh-zoh*	zoo

Memory Game Cards

www.ingramcontent.com/pod-product-compliance
Lightning Source LLC
Chambersburg PA
CBHW062107090426
42741CB00015B/3350